SIMPLE MACHINES

Ramps

by Kay Manolis

BELLWETHER MEDIA · MINNEAPOLIS, MN

Note to Librarians, Teachers, and Parents:

Blastoff! Readers are carefully developed by literacy experts and combine standards-based content with developmentally appropriate text.

Level 1 provides the most support through repetition of high-frequency words, light text, predictable sentence patterns, and strong visual support.

Level 2 offers early readers a bit more challenge through varied simple sentences, increased text load, and less repetition of high-frequency words.

Level 3 advances early-fluent readers toward fluency through increased text and concept load, less reliance on visuals, longer sentences, and more literary language.

Level 4 builds reading stamina by providing more text per page, increased use of punctuation, greater variation in sentence patterns, and increasingly challenging vocabulary.

Level 5 encourages children to move from "learning to read" to "reading to learn" by providing even more text, varied writing styles, and less familiar topics.

Whichever book is right for your reader, Blastoff! Readers are the perfect books to build confidence and encourage a love of reading that will last a lifetime!

This edition first published in 2010 by Bellwether Media, Inc.

No part of this publication may be reproduced in whole or in part without written permission of the publisher. For information regarding permission, write to Bellwether Media, Inc., Attention: Permissions Department, Post Office Box 19349, Minneapolis, MN 55419.

Library of Congress Cataloging-in-Publication Data
Manolis, Kay.
   Ramps / by Kay Manolis.
      p. cm. — (Blastoff! readers. Simple machines)
   Includes bibliographical references and index.
   Summary: "Simple text, full color photographs, and illustrations introduce beginning readers to the basic principles of ramps. Developed by literary experts for students in grades 2 through 5"—Provided by publisher.
   ISBN 978-1-60014-346-5 (hardcover : alk. paper)
   1. Inclined planes—Juvenile literature. I. Title.

TJ147.M2275 2010
621.8–dc22   2009008271

Contents

What Is a Ramp?

Have you ever seen people unload a truck? They move furniture and other heavy items down a **ramp**. A ramp is a **simple machine**. A simple machine has few or no moving parts. A ramp makes it easier to move heavy objects between high and low places. These objects are called **loads**.

Moving a load from one place to another is called **work**. You use **force** when you do work. Force causes objects to start moving, stop moving, or change direction. You use force when you walk down stairs. The amount of force you use is called **effort**.

How Ramps Work

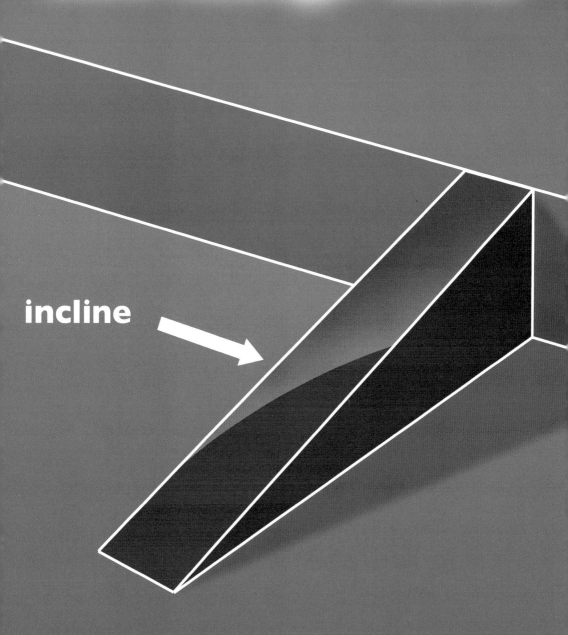

incline

The ramp is the only simple machine that does not move to make work easier. A ramp has a slanted surface. This means that one end is higher than the other end. The slanted surface is called an **incline**. Lifting a heavy object can be difficult. It is easier to move it up a ramp.

fun fact

A dump truck creates an inclined plane when it lifts up its bed. The materials in the bed slide out because of the inclined plane!

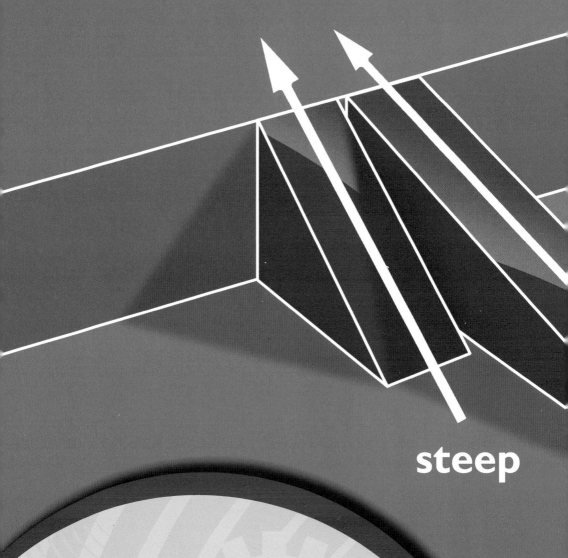

steep

Inclines can be short and steep.
It takes less time to move a load
up a short, steep ramp, but you
use more effort.

Inclines can be long and **shallow**.
It takes more time to move a load
up a long, shallow ramp, but you
use less effort.

fun fact

The length of a ramp is
called the run. The height
of a ramp is called the rise.

shallow

Examples of Ramps

People use many types of ramps to make work easier. Ladders are ramps. Firefighters use them when they put out fires. You use a ramp when you climb stairs.

People who use wheelchairs rely on ramps to enter and exit buildings. Wheelchairs can go up wheelchair ramps easily because they are long and shallow.

Mountain roads are ramps that help cars drive over steep mountains. Instead of going straight up and down a mountain, these roads wind around them. It takes more time to drive over mountains on winding roads than it would to drive straight over them. However, car engines do not have to work as hard on a winding road. A car engine has to work very hard to drive straight up a steep mountain!

Ramps are also used in many sports. Motorcycle racing is a sport where people ride bikes around a racetrack. The racetrack includes many ramps called jumps. The ramps send the bikes high in the air as the riders jump off of them. Riders soar higher off of steep ramps, but go farther off of shallower ramps.

! fun fact
Robbie Maddison jumped a motorcycle 351 feet (107 meters) off of a ramp in 2008!

People use ramps every day in different places. People park their cars in parking ramps. They drive slowly from one level to the next in search of a parking space.

Children use ramps at a playground. They play on ramps each time they climb the monkey bars or go down a slide.

Ramps and Complex Machines

Ramps are often parts of **complex machines**. A complex machine is made of two or more simple machines that work together.

A roller coaster is a complex machine you ride at an amusement park. The roller coaster track is a ramp. You climb to the top of it so you can race down the other side at high speeds!

Glossary

complex machine—a machine made of two or more simple machines that work together

effort—the amount of force needed to move an object from one place to another

force—a push or pull that causes an object to move, change its direction, or stop moving

incline—a surface that has one end higher than the other

load—an object moved by a machine

ramp—a simple machine used to move loads from one level to another

shallow—anything that is not steep

simple machine—a machine that has few or no moving parts

work—to move a load from one place to another

To Learn More

AT THE LIBRARY

Gardner, Robert. *Sensational Science Projects with Simple Machines*. Berkley Heights, N.J.: Enslow, 2006.

Hewitt, Sally. *Machines We Use*. New York, N.Y.: Children's Press, 1998.

Royston, Angela. *Ramps and Wedges*. Chicago, Ill.: Heinemann, 2001.

ON THE WEB

Learning more about simple machines is as easy as 1, 2, 3.

1. Go to www.factsurfer.com.

2. Enter "simple machines" into the search box.

3. Click the "Surf" button and you will see a list of related Web sites.

With factsurfer.com, finding more information is just a click away.

Index

The images in this book are reproduced through the courtesy of: Bogdan Ionescu, front cover; Drive Images / Alamy, pp. 4-5; Monkey Business Images, pp. 6-7; Jon Eppard, pp. 8-9, 10-11; Jack Dagley Photography, p. 12; Ron Bailey, p. 13; G P Bowater pp. 14-15; Randy Miramontez, pp. 16-17; Susan Reed, p. 18; Justin Baile / Getty Images, p. 19; Rommel / Masterfile, pp. 20-21.